thought-filled

LITTLE PONDERINGS

A Collection Of Accidental Inspiration

thought-filled
LITTLE PONDERINGS

A Collection Of Accidental Inspiration

by
Meara McMains

(C) 2017 by Meara McMains

Published by **MERAKI HOUSE PUBLISHING INC.**

All rights reserved. This book or any portion thereof may not be reproduced or used in any manner whatsoever without the express written permission of the publisher except for the use of brief quotations in a book review.

For any information regarding permission contact Meara McMains via

mearamcmains@yahoo.com

Printed in the United States of America
First publication, 2017.

Paperback: 978-1-988364-14-8

Book cover design by
www.designisreborn.com

Dedication

*In honour of the one who unknowingly
inspired it all.*

*To all the encouragers and the neighsayers, you were all
navigational beacons, so thank you.*

*To my darling parents for putting up with their dreamer
of a daughter all this time.*

*To my brothers, grandparents, aunt, and friends for taking
active interest in the progress
of this dream.*

SO much love and many, many hugs to you all!

Contents

Grow	13
Love	37
Change	51
The Breaks	67
Enough	83
Dreams	95
Be The Light	105
The Journey	123
Celebrate	139
Further Tidbits	157
Conclusion	171
About the Author	173

MEARA MCMAINS

Introduction

These days, first world Americans seem to want a step by step guide on how to improve their lives. Everywhere you look there's a top ten list of how-to's: ten steps to lose weight without dieting, ten steps to feel better fast, ten ways to get better sleep. You name it, in the name of self-improvement, it has a list—or maybe even a book.

Well, friends, that is NOT what this collection is about. I firmly believe that you don't need me, of all people, telling you how to improve your own life.

I'm convinced you are the only expert on the subject and that you already possess all the tools you need to manifest your own improvements.

This is simply a collection of words and phrases combined together in specific manifestations to warm the heart and ignite the soul—words that brought comfort to my own heart in the midst of some of life's yucky bits. I believe words contain their own powerful magic.

That being said, please keep in mind that these words were created out of a certain experience within a certain time frame of my life. If some of them resonate with you, great! If not, that's great too. Maybe they will at another time. One never knows during this great journey that is the human experience. Regardless, I am sending so much light and love and many hugs to all of those who might stumble across these words. May they bring peace to your heart and joy and solace to your soul.

Please use this book as it calls to you, whether that means reading a blurb a day or simply keeping it on hand as a dose of heart chocolate for the yucky times. These words are now yours to absorb and share.

Grow

Choose happy. Choose growth. Choose progress.

Live with intention: the intention of taking every opportunity to learn how to become a better version of yourself.

Keep working.
Keep moving forward.
You'll only get stronger.

**If you can't let go of something yet, if you're not over it, then it's not over. Whatever it is, it has more to teach you.
Dig deeper.**

YOU CAN'T CHANGE A PERSON. HOWEVER, YOU CAN CHANGE YOUR PERSPECTIVE AND EXPECTATIONS OF WHAT PERTAINS TO A RELATIONSHIP WITH A PERSON.

People will create and stay entrenched in their own misery. Luckily, it's not your responsibility to save them, only they can do that. As for you, fly higher. Life has prepared you to soar.

Life is not about not making mistakes. It's about what you do with them. It's about the lessons you take away from them. The ways in which you assess and analyze your character and face the very humanistic nature of your existence. You are perfectly flawed. Humble and noble. Right and wrong. A beautiful dichotomy of attributes. Each day fall in love with the beautiful mess that is uniquely you.

Challenge every single *"I could never do that"* thought that's lurking inside your mind.

The magic in life resides beyond the confines of the norm.
Dare to grow.

*No regrets. Not one single one.
Life is not about not making mistakes.
In fact, it's a little about getting messy. And it's about what you do with those mistakes; it's about how you face them. It's about owning your side of the shit, not taking responsibility for someone else's choices, and how you grow through all of that. Your mistakes do not prove your lack of worth.
You are inherently worthy.*

**When you turn your focus to your own growth and building your own strength, when you turn your focus to the process instead of the product, you give the magic moments a chance to reveal themselves—
often when you least expect it.**

Maybe you didn't make it to your goal today, but you made progress. Be proud of yourself. Celebrate small victories. Another step of your journey is mastered. Keep breathing and keep moving forward.

Surrendering entirely is sacrificing your own power. I don't think that's what the concept of surrendering is about. I think the point of surrendering is to surrender the how and the expectations associated. Put what you want out there and expect it. Trust in it. Believe that there's no other option. But then what you release, what you let go of, what you surrender is the control piece which displays as the how. Step back. Relax.
Watch the magic. Let it be easy.

Perhaps the key in this life is to get comfortable with the uncomfortable and to let your light shine NO MATTER WHAT. When people try and break you or hold you back (which they will), let it be your motivation to propel yourself even higher in order to steer clear of their drama. YOU are a radiant being of light. Soar like the god/goddess you are. Don't hold back. The world NEEDS you, exactly as you are.

What if what you're perceiving as your ending is really just the beginning? Caterpillar to butterfly. What if what you're perceiving as your weakness is in fact where your greatest strength lies? Spread your wings. Fly. Trust that you can.

Ponderings on strength:

It's interesting that when it comes to developing physical strength we expect there to be some pain involved. If you decide to take on a new form of exercise, you expect to be physically sore the next day. But then when it comes to emotional strength, we, as a culture, tend to avoid the painful parts at all costs. We are a culture infiltrated with avoidance. Movies, sports, television, social media, and the internet are all utilized for avoidance of the hard/yucky emotions.

The thing is, the only way to get through those yucky feeling emotions is to work straight through the middle of them. By avoiding them, you're only welcoming them back into your life in a different form. The only way to truly get over something is to work straight through the juicy centre of it.

Find the place of discomfort and lean into it just a little bit more. That's where you find release. Patience. Flexibility. Growth.

When you're patient with your process, absolutely anything is possible.

It's possible that the best retaliation toward those who you feel have hurt you is to let them be, and use the momentum to propel yourself further forward. Handle your side with grace and authenticity, and then let loose and fly. Rise above the conflict, the haters, and the heartbreakers. Once you get to a certain height, all the negativity will naturally sluff away because it cannot exist in the place where you have grown.

They'll regret losing you; there's no doubt about that. But your responsibility is to your own self and to be the best you that you can possibly be. And it's in those moments that you find out you are capable of far more than you ever knew. Unbreakable.

Explore. Experiment. Test your limits. Push your boundaries. Grow. Keep growing. Keep moving forward. Never stop. Never settle. Find you. Be you. Nurture your inner child. Laugh. Laugh a lot. Be meticulous about who you choose to share your energy with. Choose love. Love hard. There is only love.

Everyone experiences emotional discomfort. The foolish point the finger of blame. The wise look inward and ask, "now what can I learn?"

No, darling. You are not flawed. You are perfectly imperfect exactly as you are. Been through some shit? Yep. Have some scars? Probably. In need of some healing? Likely. But NOT flawed.

Love

They say love is a risk. But perhaps not as much when you're completely whole already. They say love is a game. But perhaps not so much a game as it is mere existence. You ARE love.

In order to truly love another unconditionally, you must first find the darkest of your own dark and learn to love that. Only when you love all sides of yourself unconditionally can you learn to love another freely.

Falling in love often doesn't work out the way we wish. Perhaps it's time we learn to rise in love.

"Love thy neighbor as thyself."
Not a bad concept. In fact, probably a great one. But perhaps we are missing a step. We forget to teach our children how to love themselves first, so we wind up with a society full of grownups with some serious limitations to loving each other. In order to be able to love each other truly unconditionally and experience love from others unconditionally, we must FIRST dig deep and learn to love our selves unconditionally. UNCONDITIONALLY.

Meaning, it is necessary to cozy up with our yucky bits and learn to love them just as much as the traits that make us proud. Own our mistakes, but don't allow them to own us. We are all beautifully unique, perfectly flawed individuals here to have our own unique presence and experience on this great earth.

In the process of learning how to love your darkness, you will ultimately find your greatest light.

It's freedom, it's hope for the future, it's unspoken communication, it's a relentless pursuit to be better than yesterday, it's commitment, it's an unbreakable bond, it's sanctuary, it's a new lesson learned every single day, it's perseverance, and it's resilience—it's love.

Believe in hugs. Hugs contain a powerful magic of healing. Believe in love.

Remember when people are judging you, what that really represents is a reflection of a lack of love for themselves. Likewise, when you find yourself judging others, take note that what it s reflecting is a lack of love within yourself.

Sometimes the most loving thing we can do is let go: let go of doubt, let go of fear, let go of control, let go of expectation, let go of relationships.

"Go where you're celebrated, not merely tolerated."

— *Paul F. Davis. Go where the love is.*

I took the chance to navigate through the darkest and dustiest depths of my own soul, and you know what I found there?
I found beauty. I found strength.
I found light. I found peace.
I found joy. I found abundance.
I found love.

Change

MEARA MCMAINS

Take chances. Make a change.
Don't underestimate yourself.
Never settle for ordinary;
you deserve extraordinary.

Finding balance is harder on uneven ground. Sometimes life can be a little turbulent. It doesn't mean you are not strong. It doesn't mean you're not enough. It simply means you're gaining strength and wisdom in new ways. You're growing. You're preparing to fly.

SOMETIMES YOU NEED TO TURN YOUR WORLD UPSIDE DOWN IN ORDER TO GAIN SOME PERSPECTIVE.

The thing is, no matter what your evaluation of someone's character may be, it's inaccurate. If you happen to think someone is a "good person," they're likely to disappoint. If you think someone is a "bad person," they likely have some favourable qualities that are going unrecognized. The truth is, every single person on this planet is simply doing the best they can navigating this human experience, within the context of their current level of understanding their own truths. That puts us ALL on an equal playing field—every single one of us.

What if we changed our perspective from what our bodies look like to what our bodies are capable of? Think of what a difference that slight alteration would make. What would our society look like if we all stood in amazement of the miracle that is our body?

Perhaps one of the hardest things to do is finding a way to keep your heart open once it's been broken. Our defences want to shut that sucker down, wall it off, keep all the pain away. But in doing that, you're also shutting out life's continuous gifts. Sure it's OK to shut 'er down a bit upon initial impact, like we put band aids on new wounds to keep the germs out and not let that gaping gash get infected. But at some point, preferably sooner rather than later, it's absolutely vital to the regeneration of your spirit to open that big, glorious, loving heart of yours to the world and show yourself (and everyone else) that you're stronger than the pain.

There are no positive or negative emotions. There are simply emotions. Any given emotion is simply an opportunity for growth. It's a navigational beacon. It's simply an opportunity to analyze, assess, and discover why you feel that way. We are so trained to believe that emotions like anger, frustration, or sadness are somehow negative. Perhaps in abundance there's some truth to that.

"*Everything in moderation, including moderation.*"
— **Oscar Wilde**

But perhaps it's simply time for a change in perspective.
Life is going to happen with or without your permission.
Might as well relax and learn to enjoy the ride. Go with the flow.

Sometimes it's simply time for a change. Fear and fight it, or embrace it and take the opportunity to learn and grow.

Life is full of fluctuations and cycles. Go with the flow.

Don't let circumstances deter you.
Find your balance and breathe.

It's worthwhile to learn how to fall on your face every once in a while. Simply laugh it off and try again.

MEARA MCMAINS

The Breaks

Karma.

We tend to think of it as a bad thing. As if life will kick your ass for the things you've done "wrong." But maybe that's not it at all. Sure, when karma appears in your life it probably feels yucky. You're probably facing a situation that wasn't particularly pleasant in the first place. But I think of karma as an opportunity. What's happening is you're scraping that emotional scar or scab back open; so yeah, it probably hurts a little bit (or maybe a lotta bit). But here's where the opportunity lies. It's open again and that's when the light can get in. Penetrate deep into that wound. Cleanse it from the inside out. The opportunity lies in handling the situation in a totally different way. Integrating the lesson that comes with it and allowing the light of truth to finally heal the wound in a way that's healthy for your growth and human experience. The result is completely soul nourishing if you allow yourself to dig deep and "go there."

We are so afraid of self-destruction; I can't help but wonder why. Burn, baby, burn. Burn yourself up for something you love. It's a win-win for you, really. Things work out the way you wanted? Great! It doesn't? Great! Let yourself burn into that pile of ash. Snuggle in close with it. Then use it to fertilize your next you. It's only when you completely disintegrate yourself that you have the divine opportunity to completely recreate yourself.

Take your time. Go slow. Make every single aspect of your life **EXACTLY** what **YOU** want. Burn yourself up again and again if you need to. Keep recreating your story until your dreams come true. You are capable. You are strong. You are enough. You are way beyond enough, as a matter of fact.

**WHEN YOU LOSE YOURSELF,
THAT'S ALSO WHERE YOU HAVE
THE OPPORTUNITY TO FIND
YOUR TRUE SELF.
OR RE-CREATE YOURSELF.
OR RE-INVENT YOURSELF.**

Your weakness IS your strength. What you perceive as your weakness is what makes you human. And what makes you human is what makes you relatable to mankind. And dang it, we need YOU exactly as you are. Embrace it. Shine on.

Heartbreak is where the magic moments lie. The breaks are where the light gets in. The chances to surprise yourself. Sometimes even better is complete annihilation. Complete self-annihilation creates opportunity for complete rebirth or regeneration of oneself.

Everything is perfect and nothing matters. Everything is perfect does not mean that everything is easy. In fact, sometimes it's quite the opposite of easy. It simply means that everything is exactly as it needs to be. However, trusting that it is as it needs to be makes it that much easier, leading you straight back to perfect.

Heartbreak is simply an opportunity to root down deeper and fly higher than you ever thought possible.

Maybe it's not your heart that's broken. Maybe it's your ego. How easily we get the two confused. We feel broken when something doesn't work out the way we want or imagine and we accuse our heart of the pain. But perhaps it's really just ego throwing a temper tantrum and our heart steering us in the direction of our dreams.

It's amazing what life's ass-kickings will wring out of you if you let it. It's a bit of a paradox, really. We think (or at least I did) that by fighting the yucky feelings, by holding them off with swift and true punches, that we appear strong and therefore we must be a strong person. But that's not it at all. It's when you allow yourself to feel every little nuance of a feel: every pain, every hurt, every betrayal, every perceived abandonment, every hardship, every vulnerability, and every insecurity. When you recognize each layer of masks of the image(s) you wear to face the world and learn to face yourself. It's in the unraveling of the paradoxes of the true you—that's where you will discover your true strength. You must dig down to rise up. As above, so below.

One of the most beautiful spaces you can be is broken. When you're broken, you're open. When you're open, you're receptive. Be brave enough to break yourself open over and over again, and allow yourself to receive everything the universe has to offer you today. Dig deep into the gushy bits of you. It's a beautiful day. You're a beautiful you.

Sometimes divine miracles show up in the form of perceived great loss.

Enough

No matter how hard your situation might seem right now, take confidence in knowing that you find yourself in it because you are enough. You are strong enough, you are brave enough, you are worthy enough, you are fierce enough, you have faith enough, and you are light enough.

Face your fears, confront your demons.

YOU ARE ENOUGH.

What if it's neither good nor bad? What if it simply is. It's just a thing. It's just an experience. It's just a moment. It happens, and it will pass, just as the moment before did. What if it's us who give it the power of "good" or "bad" when we apply the label? What if it's all simply a piece of your story? Nothing more, nothing less. Except that it's YOUR story. And that in itself makes it an epic tale. Embrace your journey. Love it. Cherish its smolder. Trust your process. Let go of what no longer serves you, whether it be a system of beliefs, a relationship, a job, or anything in between. Project ultimate positivity and it will radiate itself back to you. Expect miracles. Believe in magic. Fall in love with every single piece of your epic tale of discovering your own greatness. "It's all just a pigment of your hallucination."

YOU ARE ENOUGH, AND YOU ARE MOST DEFINITELY STRONG ENOUGH. KEEP MOVING FORWARD.

*Breathe. Surrender.
Over and over again.
Trust that your entire existence is
supported for your greatest good.*

Believe in your own strength.
You are your own magic.
You are enough.

Positives and negatives are illusions of the human condition.

No matter what, the ONLY one in charge of healing your heart is yourself. And the only way to heal it successfully is to confront your hurts head-on with unapologetic authenticity. Handle yourself gently. You're doing better than you know.

The glass is neither half full nor half empty. Regardless of your perspective, the glass itself simply exists. As is. Same goes for life. It's not a positive or negative life. There are no positive or negative experiences. There are no positive or negative emotions.
They simply exist. As is.

Quietly pursue that which speaks to your heart.

Today, let your faith be bigger than your fear. Crack your heart open for the zillionth time, and trust your inner knowing. Believe in yourself.
Believe in your dreams.
It's all happening. Now.
Manifest your own destiny.

Relax. Breathe. Everything is unfolding exactly as intended.

Know your worth, *AND* know that you are worthy. Know that you are worthy of all of your dreams.

Don't believe them! It's a trap! The truth is, you absolutely CAN be anything that you want to be. You absolutely don't have to do things you don't want to do. You don't have to be a mindless drone in a mind-numbing society. You absolutely have something unique and of value to offer this world. Guaranteed.

Doubt your own self-imposed, self-limiting beliefs. Trust the process. You're stronger than you know. Defy gravity. Get yourself ready to fly.

It's possible that we are entering a day and age where we will find that there is strength in vulnerability, where you find that your own divine power lies in openness and authenticity, where you live in reckless abandon to your own true nature, and where abundance is to be found within the autonomy of your own world experience.

Be The Light

THERE ARE PLENTY OF PEOPLE IN THIS WORLD WHO SETTLE FOR ADEQUATELY MEDIOCRE LIVES. RISE ABOVE IT. DARE TO DREAM. BE BRAVE ENOUGH TO GO FOR IT. KEEP FIGHTING FOR YOUR OWN SELF; BY NATURE IT WILL INSPIRE OTHERS TO DO THE SAME. LIVE PASSIONATELY. LIVE AUTHENTICALLY. LIVE FULLY.

Love always wins. Though I believe this to be true, perhaps a lot of us have a skewed idea of what love is. What we currently have in place is a system of checks and balances, of expectations and consequences, of fear and control.

We say we love our children unconditionally, but do we really? We often have many expectations for them to adhere when they're children and much less when they hit school age and work age. We reward and punish them according to our own expectations and sometimes prioritize that over their happiness or general wellbeing. We also put expectations on our relationships, as if our very existence or what we are willing to do for another automatically earns us a certain kind of treatment. We say that loving someone is to want what's best for them, but boy, do we form our own opinions about what's best for each person in our world. So what is love? You ARE love. You exist to be and embody love. You are love incarnate, radiating like a beacon.

The trick is to delve into your own existence far enough to release all of our social conditionings, and see yourself for the radiant beauty that you truly are.

When you make the conscious decision to push your boundaries and break free from your own comfort zones with some regularity, the whole world becomes your playground.

Sometimes the most beautiful people in this world are the most considerably misunderstood.

You can change the past by changing your perception of the past. It doesn't change the events themselves, but it can change the hold those events have on you.

Living a positive life does not mean suppressing the aspects we consider to be negative. In fact, it requires embracing and loving those parts of ourselves as well.

Sometimes when you do the brave thing, the rewards you receive in return are too numerous to count.

I'M NOT SURE I BELIEVE IN DARKNESS IN A PERSON. I BELIEVE THERE ARE PEOPLE WHO SIMPLY HAVE YET TO FIND THEIR OWN LIGHT.

Investing in a child is never, ever a waste.

Today, choose to shine.

CHILDREN ARE EARTH'S LITTLE ANGELS.

Life is amazing. Every single day. Find new heights. Create new depths. Explore every caveat of the world around you. Marvel in its wonder. Rejoice in its majesty. Cherish its love and laughter. Breathe and trust that everything is perfect just the way it is. And love. Love hard. Love always. There is only love.

Sometimes the brighter you shine, the harder people try and stomp out your light. Stay positive, my darlings, no matter what. Keep your heart open, and don't ever dim your light.

"Why fit in when you were born to stand out?"
— **Dr. Seuss**

Stand for what you believe in. Defend those who need a voice. Fight the good fight.

The thing about it is, in order to get to your highest high, you must allow yourself the experience of your lowest low. You have to move through the grit to get to the glory. You must learn to fall gracefully before you can fly. Otherwise, what good is it to get to the top if you can't fully appreciate the value of the experience?

Explore your world from every possible angle.

There is no destination point, really. It's all about the process. Learn to love the process and you'll learn to love life.

**TAKE HEART, DEAR ONE.
WHEREVER YOU ARE ON
YOUR JOURNEY, IT IS EXACTLY
WHERE YOU NEED TO BE.**

Life's journey is hard. REALLY hard. In fact, it's the hardest thing you will ever do. But it's absolutely worth the climb. Keep climbing. Once you reach the top, you'll be prepared to fly.

Things they don't teach you:

They don't tell you that you'll have a handful of spot on, ideal days in your life, a handful of days where survival is success, and a whole bunch of days that range somewhere in between. They don't tell you that you'll be navigating through an endless ocean of emotion from a wide variety of individual personalities, going through a countless array of circumstances— most of which are not within an individual's locus of control.

"My favorite animal is the turtle. The reason is that in order for the turtle to move, it has to stick its neck out. There are going to be times in your life when you're going to have to stick your neck out. There will be challenges and instead of hiding in a shell, you have to go out and meet them."

— Ruth Westheimers

I happened to come across a turtle, sticking its little neck out, trying to cross the road—a pretty vulnerable and precarious situation for a turtle. I made the choice (maybe wrong, maybe right) that the turtle would be better served by being relocated to the pond from which it had surely come. This seemed to me like a reminder of the other side of this quote. Yes, by all means, stick your neck out. Take risks. Move forward with meaning. But remember, it's also OK from time to time to tuck into your turtle shell and allow your community to lovingly support you. Ultimately, the turtle was transported back to the pond and allowed to return to freedom.

"You must love in such a way that the person you love feels free."
— Thach Nhat Hanh

There's a lot you can learn if you're willing to take a walk alone in the woods. Same can be said if you're willing to take a walk within and explore your own soul.

Create a life that you don't feel the need to dream of an escape from. One where you're completely in love with every second of every day, even the tough stuff. One where every situation and every relationship brings more growth and positive energy to your world than negativity. Fully invest and create a life worth living.

By all means, stay in your comfort zone. Be the emperor/ess of your own little world. Or maybe try pushing your own limits.
Discover new boundaries.
The whole world is your play place.
A world of discovery awaits.

To me, one of the most beautiful things about the journey is the continuous opportunities you have to surprise yourself.

It's beautiful because I found it along my journey.

Celebrate

MEARA MCMAINS

They say that happiness is a choice. Although I agree to an extent, I'm going to offer a slight modification to that concept.

'Cause you know what? Shit happens. Sometimes it sucks. Sometimes it really, really sucks. Sometimes life's really, really hard. Loss happens. And it's OK to be sad about it. In fact, it's a necessary part of the process. I'm going to say that again because I don't think we hear that message enough in our escapist, Neverland of a society. IT'S OK TO BE SAD. But here's where the choice happens.

I think it's important to allow yourself to be sad for a while. For whatever reason. Or even for no reason at all. Feeling sad is part of the whole human experience. But the choice is in whether or not you allow it to take over. The choice is whether you decide to keep living, and this is where you have the opportunity to show your strength.

Sometimes the right answer might be to just keep going through the motions in life. Keep breathing, and ONWARD! Eventually, over time, you will work through the sad and you WILL find your happy again—naturally, without forcing it or faking it—and THAT's when you know it's genuine. Be gentle with yourself, but also be encouraging and keep moving forward.

Reminder:

Anything is possible.
Don't take anything (especially yourself) too seriously.

Crack yourself open. Let yourself break.
That s where the magic happens every damn time.
What s holding you back? Probably fear.
What happens when you acknowledge it, greet it,
maybe even give it a little hug and say, "I see you
there, fear?" What happens when you don t deny it
or dismiss it or hide it or hide from it? MAGIC.
Growth. Every single time. Magic may happen in
the form of the teeniest step of progress, but it s
magic nonetheless. Love and hug every damn day.
But first and foremost, love yourself!
Celebrate small victories!

Know that you are limitless.
Nothing is impossible.
Some things just take
a little extra time.

**Pssst, I have a secret.
You know that thing you wish you could do with your life? You absolutely can do it. You are more than capable. You are enough. You are more than enough. You are overflowing with enough-ness.
Set an intention.
Breathe. Believe. Receive.**

"You are the best."

This is something I tell my dog every single day, and you know what? He truly is. He embodies best-ness. He has lived up to that expectation and then some. As I was reflecting about this, I realized that perhaps part of why he is the best is that he gets the concept reinforced every single day. He has no reason to believe otherwise. He doesn't have the internal dialogue refuting the fact that he is the best. What kind of magic would we bring to the world if we all believed that about everyone we encounter in this life? What kind of magic would we bring to this world if we all believed this about ourselves?

You know what? YOU deserve a cookie today. Why? Because you're here. You're breathing. You showed up. You faced another day. Life is a weird, crazy ride and YOU checked off another piece of it. Celebrate small victories! Love yourself first!

"Courage is not the absence of fear, but rather the judgment that something else is more important than fear."
~ **Ambrose Redmoon**

To continue to move forward on our life's journey, it becomes vital to learn to face our fears. Fears come in all shapes and sizes, with emphasis on internal and external forces. But ultimately, fear is energy, just like everything else. Nothing more and nothing less. To successfully navigate our path, learning to use fear as a tool or a guide can be greatly beneficial. Acknowledge its presence. Face it. Let it lead you into the unknown. That, my angels, is growth.

And within that growth lies infinite love and abundance.
Surrender to each moment, over and over again until you finally see that nothing needs to be different. Ever. Everything is always exactly as it needs to be.

Trust your own strength.
Find your balance. Fly.

Live it. Love it. Hike it. Climb it.
Relish it. Absorb it. Cherish it.
Breathe it. Freeze it. Burn it.
Bruise it. Experience it.
Every single satiating,
juicy nuance of it.

The miracle you are seeking lies within you.

LESSON LEARNED FROM EVERY SUPERHERO:

ONLY THE LIGHT QUESTIONS ITS OWN INNER DARKNESS. THE DARKNESS SIMPLY ASSUMES ITS OWN LIGHT.

Be brave enough and bold enough to create and live out the life your soul desires. Never settle. Always grow. Never underestimate yourself. You are at home amongst the stars. You are limitless. Love. Love hard. Keep loving. Learn to love yourself first. Live in bliss every single day.

You are truly a limitless being. The only things holding you back are your own limited thought patterns and perceived realities. You are more powerful than you could possibly imagine.

Further Tidbits

She/he should make you tremble. You'll find the entire universe in her/his eyes. She/he embraces weakness as strength, inspires growth, challenges ambitions and world views. She's/he's a perfect storm wrapped in the warm embrace of a thousand smiles. Delight in her/his power for that power also resides within you.

People deserve to hear your truths. Let your light drive out their darkness.

I think often when we take diligent care of our mental health, our physical health follows. It is all connected. Heal your mind, heal your body, and heal your life.

Radiate vibrant authenticity.

Everywhere you look you can find advice on how to improve your life: how to lose weight, how to be happier, how to find love...it's all kind of absurd to me. Here's a thought: dig deep, look within yourself, figure out what it would take to fall intensely in love with your own life, be brave enough to make the necessary changes, and perhaps EVERYTHING else might just fall into place.

IN THIS SOCIETY, WE GLORIFY DRAMA AND CONFLICT, AND THEN WONDER WHY WE CAN'T FIND PEACE.

Never fear. Your light outshines the darkness any day.

There is no such thing as failure as long as you try.

Death, dying, mortality, and the afterlife for whatever it s worth, here are my two cents on the subject. Find a truth that brings peace and comfort to your heart, no matter what that truth may be. Grasp onto it. Hold it with all our might. Own that shit. Cause let s be real about it, it really doesn t matter. Not to be a Debbie Downer or anything, but reality is, no matter what you choose to believe in, we re all going to die anyway. And none of us REALLY know what s going to happen beyond that. So, might as well choose to believe in something that you can be at peace with during the time you ve got.

If you want to grow into being a certain type of human, surround yourself with that kind of human. If you want to become a runner, hang out with runners. If you want to become a reader, hang out with readers. If you want to become patient and loving, hang out with patient and loving people. If you want to become an asshole, hang out with assholes. Consciously or not, the people who surround yourself with rub off on you.

Repeat after me:

I am human. I am flawed. I own my mistakes, but I do not allow them to own me. My mistakes are not my identity (but neither are my accomplishments).

Conclusion

I do hope these words have brought some peace to your heart. Remember, your experience is yours and yours alone. Your journey is deeply personal and hopefully as enriching and fulfilling as you wish it to be.

Keep in mind, ultimately, there is only love.

May this dream empower some minds and lighten some hearts. Go out and be a light in the world this week.

Meara McMains
- AUTHOR -

Meara is a San Antonio, Texas native. Raised on tacos and hugs, she has spent most of her professional life being inspired by young minds. A teacher by trade, she had the unique opportunity to pursue and explore many passions including horseback riding, violin and yoga. Currently working to complete her masters in counseling, she intends to pursue doctoral studies in counselor education and combine her passion for people and yoga into a culture and practice of healing. You can find her at www.mnmyoga.com. Photo credit to the beautiful Natasha Hagerty.

MERAKI HOUSE
PUBLISHING

*Publishing with
Soul, Creativity & Love*

Meraki House Publishing, founded in 2015 has established its brand as an independent virtual publishing house designed to suit your needs as the Author, delivering the highest quality design, writing and editorial, publishing and marketing services to ensure your success.

"Where your needs as an Author have become ours as an independent Publishing House."

WWW.MERAKIHOUSE.COM

In partnership with
www.designisreborn.com

Copyright 2016, Meraki House Publishing

Marnie Kay, Founder & CEO
marniekay.com

www.ingramcontent.com/pod-product-compliance
Lightning Source LLC
Chambersburg PA
CBHW060525080526
44586CB00012B/623